Frog Tales

Dona Foucault
Art by Lydia Ferron

Literacy Consultants
David Booth • Kathleen Corrigan

Spencer, Paige, and Dad
were going to the pond.
They wanted to catch fish.

"Are you kids ready?" Dad asked.

"I have the net," Spencer said.

"I have the bucket," Paige said.

"Then let's get going!" Dad said.

At the pond,
Spencer saw a turtle.

Paige chased
butterflies with the net.

Dad tripped and got all wet.
But nobody saw any fish.

4

"Look!" said Paige.

Dad and Spencer went over to see what Paige was pointing at.

"What are those?" Paige asked.

"Those look like fish eggs," Dad said.

"Where is the mommy fish?"
Spencer asked.

"Why isn't she watching her eggs?"
asked Paige.

"Not all animals watch their eggs,"
replied Dad.

"Can we take the eggs home?"
Paige asked.

"They have to stay here," said Dad.
"But we can check on them every day."

The next day, they went back
to the same spot.

The eggs were gone!

"The eggs have hatched," said Dad.

"Look!" Spencer shouted.
"Tiny fish babies!"

"Dad!" Paige said.
"These fish look funny!"

"These aren't fish.
They are tadpoles!" Dad said.

"Tadpoles?" Spencer asked.

"Yes," said Dad.
"That's what you call baby frogs."

10

"They don't look like frogs," said Spencer.

"Tadpoles change a lot before
they become frogs," said Dad.

After dinner, Dad, Paige, and Spencer sat around the computer.

Tadpoles go through many changes to become frogs.

First a tadpole
has a long tail.

Then the tail
gets shorter.

Soon it will lay
its own eggs.

The tadpole
becomes a froglet.

Then the froglet
becomes a frog.

"Our tadpoles are so little now!"
Paige said.
"They're going to change
so much!"

"Yes, they will," said Dad.

Then the tail gets shorter.

"We should go back
to the pond every day.
We can watch them change,"
Dad said.

"Yes!" said Paige and Spencer.

"Maybe we will meet the frogs!"